God's Little Instruction Book for Women

HONOR
BOOKS

07 06 05 04 03   10 9 8 7 6 5 4 3 2 1

God's Little Instruction Book for Women
ISBN 1-56292-801-5
Copyright © 1996, 2003 by Honor Books
An Imprint of Cook Communications Ministries
4050 Lee Vance View
Colorado Springs, CO 80918

Manuscript prepared by W.B. Freeman Concepts,
Tulsa, Oklahoma.

Introduction

God's Little Instruction Book for Women is
a collection of dynamic quotes and sayings
spanning the wisdom of the centuries.
Each quote is accompanied by a Scripture,
with an emphasis on the practical and
spiritual experiences of today's women.
Together they offer comfort and guidance,
hope and encouragement—and even a
good laugh or two.

This book will be fun reading, yet thought-
provoking. It will challenge you to expand
your outlook and to fulfill your potential as a
woman. Whether you are active in corporate
America or in the home, these timeless
thoughts will recharge your inner being and
give you sound advice as a bonus. Enjoy your
time absorbing these pages—many of them
were written just for you!

$\mathcal{M}$y job is to take

care of the possible

and trust God

with the impossible.

They that know thy name will put
their trust in thee: for thou, LORD, hast
not forsaken them that seek thee.
Psalm 9:10

When Mother Teresa received
her Nobel Prize, she was asked,
"What can we do to promote
world peace?" She replied,
"Go home and love your family."

Let love and faithfulness never leave you;
bind them around your neck,
write them on the tablet of your heart.
Proverbs 3:3 NIV

You are never so

high as when you

are on your knees.

Humble yourselves in the sight of the Lord, and he shall lift you up.
James 4:10

Give your troubles to God:

He will be up

all night anyway.

He will not allow your foot to slip;
He who keeps you will not slumber.
Psalm 121:3 NASB

We should seize

every opportunity

to give encouragment.

Encouragement is

oxygen to the soul.

A man hath joy by the answer of
his mouth: and a word spoken
in due season, how good is it!
Proverbs 15:23

You may give

without loving,

but you cannot love

without giving.

God so loved the world, that he gave his only begotten Son, that whosoever believeth in him should not perish, but have everlasting life.
John 3:16

When I come to the

end of my rope, God is

there to take over.

I will never leave thee, nor forsake thee.
Hebrews 13:5

The Lord can do great things through those who don't care who gets the credit.

A man's pride shall bring him low: but honour shall uphold the humble in spirit.
Proverbs 29:23

What sunshine is to flowers,

smiles are to humanity.

They are but trifles, to be sure but,

scattered along life's pathway, the

good they do is inconceivable.

A happy heart makes the face cheerful.
Proverbs 15:13 NIV

$\mathcal{I}$ regret often that
$\mathcal{I}$ have spoken; never
that $\mathcal{I}$ have been silent.

*In the multitude of words there
wanteth not sin: but he that
refraineth his lips is wise.*

Proverbs 10:19

"*I* can forgive, but I cannot forget," is only another way of saying, "I will not forgive." Forgiveness ought to be like a canceled note— torn in two, and burned up, so that it never can be shown against one.

Be ye kind one to another, tenderhearted, forgiving one another, even as God for Christ's sake hath forgiven you.
Ephesians 4:32

Worry is like a rocking chair: It gives you something to do, but doesn't get you anywhere.

Casting the whole of your care [all your anxieties, all your worries, all your concerns, once and for all] on Him, for He cares for you affectionately and cares about you watchfully.

1 Peter 5:7 AMP

Look around you

and be distressed,

Look within you

and be depressed,

Look to Jesus and be at rest.

*In my distress I cried unto the LORD,
and he heard me.*
Psalm 120:1

There is no greater love than the love that holds on where there seems nothing left to hold on to.

Love never fails [never fades out or becomes obsolete or comes to an end].

1 Corinthians 13:8 AMP

*D*aily prayers will

diminish your cares.

Evening, and morning, and at noon,
will I pray, and cry aloud: and
he shall hear my voice.

Psalm 55:17

Each loving act says loud and clear, "I love you. God loves you. I care. God cares."

Beloved, let us love one another: for love is of God; and every one that loveth is born of God ... for God is love.
1 John 4:7-8

$\mathcal{I}$ have held many things in my hands and lost them all; but the things $\mathcal{I}$ have placed in *God's* hands, those $\mathcal{I}$ always possess.

I know whom I have believed, and am persuaded that he is able to keep that which I have committed unto him against that day.
2 Timothy 1:12

A good deed is never lost;

he who sows courtesy reaps

friendship, and he who plants

kindness gathers love.

Whatsoever a man soweth,
that shall he also reap....
And let us not be weary in
well doing: for in due season
we shall reap, if we faint not.
Galatians 6:7,9

$\mathcal{K}$ind words can be

short and easy to speak,

but their echoes

are truly endless.

*She opens her mouth in skillful
and godly Wisdom, and on her
tongue is the law of kindness
[giving counsel and instruction].*
Proverbs 31:26 AMP

Nothing beats love

at first sight except

love with insight.

The beginning of wisdom is this:
Get wisdom,
and whatever else you get, get insight.
Proverbs 4:7 NRSV

A house is made of walls

and beams; a home is

made of love and dreams.

Better a meal of vegetables
where there is love
than a fattened calf with hatred.
Proverbs 15:17 NIV

The best way to

hold a man is

in your arms.

The man should give his wife all that is
her right as a married woman, and the
wife should do the same for her husband.
1 Corinthians 7:3 TLB

Ninety percent of

the friction of daily life

is caused by the

wrong tone of voice.

A man finds joy in giving an apt reply—
and how good is a timely word!
Proverbs 15:23 NIV

Forgiveness is

giving love when

there is no reason to.

Blessed are the merciful,
For they shall obtain mercy.
Matthew 5:7 NKJV

Nothing is so strong as gentleness. Nothing is so gentle as real strength.

*You have also given me
the shield of Your salvation,
And Your right hand upholds me;
And Your gentleness makes me great.*
Psalm 18:35 NASB

Everyone has patience.

Successful people

learn to use it.

Let patience have her perfect work,
that ye may be perfect and entire,
wanting nothing.
James 1:4

Watch out for temptation—the more you see of it the better it looks.

Keep watching and praying that you may not come into temptation.
Mark 14:38 NASB

It is such a comfort

to drop the tangles of

life into God's hands

and leave them there.

Cast your cares on the LORD
and he will sustain you.
Psalm 55:22 NIV

Friendship improves

happiness and abates

misery, by the doubling

of our joy and the

dividing of our grief.

A friend loves at all times,
and a brother is born for adversity.
Proverbs 17:17 NIV

Everyone has an

invisible sign hanging

from his neck saying,

"Make me feel important!"

Encourage one another
and build each other up,
just as in fact you are doing.
1 Thessalonians 5:11 NIV

You cannot do a kindness

too soon, because you

never know how soon

it will be too late!

Encourage one another day after day,
as long as it is still called "Today."
Hebrews 3:13 NASB

37

Stack every bit

of criticism between

two layers of praise.

Correct, rebuke and encourage—with great patience and careful instruction.
2 Timothy 4:2 NIV

In trying times,

don't quit trying.

Let us not grow weary in well-doing,
for in due season we shall reap,
if we do not lose heart.

Galatians 6:9 RSV

*To love what you do
and feel that it matters—
how could anything
be more fun?*

**When you eat the labor of your hands,
You shall be happy, and it
shall be well with you.**
Psalm 128:2 NKJV

Life is a coin.

You can spend it any

way you wish, but you

can only spend it once.

What is your life? It is even a vapor that appears for a little time and then vanishes away.

James 4:14 NKJV

Diligence is

the mother of

good fortune.

The hand of the diligent makes rich.
Proverbs 10:4 NKJV

The most wasted of

all days is that on

which one has

not laughed.

A happy heart makes the face cheerful,
but heartache crushes the spirit.
Proverbs 15:13 NIV

You can accomplish more in one hour with God than one lifetime without Him.

Walk in wisdom ... redeeming the time.
Colossians 4:5

Courage is resistance

to fear, mastery of fear.

Not the absence of fear.

*Take up the full armor of God, so that
you will be able to resist in the evil day,
and having done everything, to
stand firm. Stand firm therefore.*
Ephesians 6:13-14 NASB

The art of being wise

is the art of knowing

what to overlook.

A man's wisdom gives him patience;
it is to his glory to overlook an offense.
Proverbs 19:11 NIV

Triumph is just

"umph" added to try.

*Let us not be weary in well doing: for in
due season we shall reap, if we faint not.*
Galatians 6:9

People don't care how much you know, until they know how much you care . . . about them.

Though I have all faith, so that I could remove mountains, and have not charity, I am nothing.
1 Corinthians 13:2

Good words are

worth much,

and cost little.

Pleasant words are a honeycomb,
Sweet to the soul and healing to the bones.
Proverbs 16:24 NASB

$\mathcal{I}$ don't know the
secret to success but the
key to failure is to
try to please everyone.

"No one can serve two masters;
for either he will hate the one
and love the other, or he will be
devoted to one and despise the other."
Matthew 6:24 NASB

No one is useless in this world who lightens the burden of it to anyone else.

*Bear ye one another's burdens,
and so fulfil the law of Christ.*
Galatians 6:2

$\mathcal{D}$o not follow where

the path may lead—

go instead where there is

no path and leave a trail.

Your ears shall hear a
word behind you, saying,
"This is the way, walk in it."
Isaiah 30:21 NKJV

There is one thing alone that

stands the brunt of life

throughout its length:

a quiet conscience.

If our hearts do not condemn us,
we have confidence before God.

1 John 3:21 NIV

53

$\mathcal{M}$y obligation is to

do the right thing.

$\mathcal{T}$he rest is in $\mathcal{G}$od's hands.

If you know that he is righteous,
you may be sure that every one
who does right is born of him.
1 John 2:29 RSV

Expect great things

from God.

Attempt great things

for God.

"He who believes in Me, the works that I do,
he will do also; and greater works than
these will he do; because I go to the Father."

John 14:12 NASB

Dost thou love life?

Then do not squander time,

for that is the stuff

life is made of.

Remember how short my time is.
Psalm 89:47

The grass may be greener

on the other side, but

it still has to be mowed.

Be content with such things as ye have.
Hebrews 13:5

Every job is a self-portrait of the person who does it. Autograph your work with excellence.

Many daughters have done well,
But you excel them all.
Proverbs 31:29 NKJV

The greatest achievements

are those that

benefit others.

"To be the greatest, be a servant."
Matthew 23:11 TLB

If a task is once begun,

never leave it till it's done.

Be the labor great or small,

do it well or not at all.

Whatever your hand finds to do,
do it with your might.
Ecclesiastes 9:10 NKJV

I would rather walk

with *God* in the dark than

go alone in the light.

*Even when walking through the dark
valley of death I will not be afraid,
for you are close beside me,
guarding, guiding all the way.*
Psalm 23:4 TLB

All our dreams can come true—if we have the courage to pursue them.

*Be strong and courageous, and act;
do not fear nor be dismayed, for
the LORD God, my God, is with you.*
1 Chronicles 28:20 NASB

*R*emember the

banana—when it left

the bunch, it got skinned.

*Not forsaking the assembling of ourselves
together, as the manner of some is; but
exhorting one another: and so much
the more, as ye see the day approaching.*
Hebrews 10:25

Decisions can take you

out of God's will but

never out of His reach.

If we are faithless,
he will remain faithful,
for he cannot disown himself.
2 Timothy 2:13 NIV

"*No*" is one of the few

words that can never

be misunderstood.

"Let your statement be 'Yes, yes' or 'No, no.'"
Matthew 5:37 NASB

Some people complain because God put thorns on roses, while others praise Him for putting roses among thorns.

Finally, brethren, whatsoever things are true, ... honest, ... just, ... pure, ... lovely, ... of good report; if there be any virtue, and if there be any praise, think on these things.

Philippians 4:8

The bridge you burn

now may be the one you

later have to cross.

If it be possible, as much as lieth in you,
live peaceably with all men.
Romans 12:18

Real friends are those who, when you've made a fool of yourself, don't feel you've done a permanent job.

[Love] bears all things, believes all things, hopes all things, endures all things. Love never fails.
1 Corinthians 13:7-8 NKJV

$\mathcal{M}$ost people wish to

serve God—but only in

an advisory capacity.

**Humble yourselves therefore under
the mighty hand of God, that he
may exalt you in due time.**
1 Peter 5:6

Conscience is God's built-in warning system. Be very happy when it hurts you. Be very worried when it doesn't.

Herein do I exercise myself, to have always a conscience void of offense toward God, and toward men.

Acts 24:16

If you don't stand for

something, you'll fall

for anything!

Ye are bought with a price: therefore
glorify God in your body, and
in your spirit, which are God's.
1 Corinthians 6:20

You should never let adversity get you down— except on your knees.

I am persuaded, that neither death, nor life, nor angels, nor principalities, nor powers, nor things present, nor things to come ... shall be able to separate us from the love of God, which is in Christ Jesus our Lord.
Romans 8:38-39

The best bridge between

hope and despair is often

a good night's sleep.

*It is vain for you to rise up early, to
sit up late, to eat the bread of sorrows:
for so he giveth his beloved sleep.*
Psalm 127:2

$\mathcal{I}$t is good to remember
that the tea kettle,
although up to its neck in
hot water, continues to sing.

*Rejoice evermore.... In every thing
give thanks: for this is the will of
God in Christ Jesus concerning you.*
1 Thessalonians 5:16,18

It's good to be a

Christian and know it,

but it's better to be a

Christian and show it!

By this shall all men know that ye are my disciples, if ye have love one to another.

John 13:35

Sorrow looks back.

Worry looks around.

Faith looks up.

Fixing our eyes on Jesus, the author and perfecter of faith, who for the joy set before Him endured the cross, despising the shame, and has sat down at the right hand of the throne of God.

Hebrews 12:2 NASB

$\mathcal{S}$ometimes we are so

busy adding up our troubles

that we forget to

count our blessings.

I will remember the works of the
LORD: surely I will remember thy
wonders of old. I will meditate also of
all thy work, and talk of thy doings.
Psalm 77:11-12

God can heal a broken heart, but He has to have all the pieces.

My son, give me thine heart.
Proverbs 23:26

Be more concerned with what God thinks about you than what people think about you.

"Seek first the kingdom of God and His righteousness, and all these things shall be added to you."
Matthew 6:33 NKJV

The best way to get

the last word is

to apologize.

If you have been trapped by what
you said, ... Go and humble yourself;
press your plea with your neighbor!

Proverbs 6:2-3 NIV

$\mathcal{F}$orget yourself for

others and others

will not forget you!

*All things whatsoever ye would that men
should do to you, do ye even so to them:
for this is the law and the prophets.*
Matthew 7:12

The secret of contentment

is the realization that

life is a gift not a right.

Godliness with contentment is great gain.
For we brought nothing into this world,
and it is certain we can carry nothing out.
1 Timothy 6:6-7

$\mathcal{T}$hose who bring sunshine

to the lives of others cannot

keep it from themselves.

Be not deceived; God is not mocked:
for whatsoever a man soweth,
that shall he also reap.
Galatians 6:7

It's the little things

in life that determine

the big things.

Thou hast been faithful over a few things,
I will make thee ruler over many things:
enter thou into the joy of thy lord.
Matthew 25:21

84

Contentment isn't getting

what we want but

being satisfied with

what we have.

*Not that I speak in respect of want: for
I have learned, in whatsoever state
I am, therewith to be content.*
Philippians 4:11

God plus one is always a majority!

If God be for us, who can be against us?
Romans 8:31

Whoever gossips

to you will be a

gossip of you.

A talebearer revealeth secrets: but he that is
of a faithful spirit concealeth the matter.
Proverbs 11:13

Jesus is a friend who knows all your faults and still loves you anyway.

God commendeth his love toward us, in that, while we were yet sinners, Christ died for us.
Romans 5:8

*Every person should
have a special cemetery lot
in which to bury the faults
of friends and loved ones.*

**Be ye kind one to another, tenderhearted,
forgiving one another, even as God
for Christ's sake hath forgiven you.**
Ephesians 4:32

A minute of thought

is worth more

than an hour of talk.

Set a watch, O LORD, before my mouth;
keep the door of my lips.
Psalm 141:3

You can win more friends with your ears than with your mouth.

Let every man be swift to hear, slow to speak, slow to wrath.

James 1:19

It's not the outlook

but the uplook

that counts.

Looking unto Jesus the author
and finisher of our faith ...
Hebrews 12:2

It isn't hard to make

a mountain out of a molehill.

Just add a little dirt.

Starting a quarrel is like breaching a dam;
so drop the matter before
a dispute breaks out.

Proverbs 17:14 NIV

The art of being

a good guest is knowing

when to leave.

**Withdraw thy foot from thy
neighbour's house; lest he be
weary of thee, and so hate thee.**
Proverbs 25:17

Jesus is a friend

who walks in when the

world has walked out.

In the world ye shall have
tribulation: but be of good cheer;
I have overcome the world.
John 16:33

Those who deserve

love the least

need it the most.

Love your enemies, bless them that
curse you, do good to them that
hate you, and pray for them which
despitefully use you, and persecute you.
Matthew 5:44

Faith is daring the soul

to go beyond what

the eyes can see.

We walk by faith, not by sight.
2 Corinthians 5:7

A critical spirit is

like poison ivy—

it only takes a little

contact to spread its poison.

Avoid worldly and empty chatter,
for it will lead to further ungodliness.
2 Timothy 2:16 NASB

Two things are hard

on the heart—running

up stairs and running

down people.

Let no corrupt communication proceed out of your mouth, but that which is good to the use of edifying, that it may minister grace unto the hearers.
Ephesians 4:29

Humor is to life what shock absorbers are to automobiles.

Our mouth was filled with laughter,
And our tongue with singing.
Then they said among the nations,
"The LORD has done great things for them."
Psalm 126:2 NKJV

$\mathscr{K}$indness is the

oil that takes the

friction out of life.

The fruit of the Spirit is ... kindness.
Galatians 5:22 NIV

Our days are identical suitcases—all the same size— but some people can pack more into them than others.

Be very careful, then, how you live— not as unwise but as wise, making the most of every opportunity.
Ephesians 5:15-16 NIV

102

To forgive is to set a prisoner free and discover the prisoner was you.

If ye forgive men their trespasses, your heavenly Father will also forgive you: But if ye forgive not men their trespasses, neither will your Father forgive your trespasses.
Matthew 6:14-15

The heart is the

happiest when it

beats for others.

Greater love hath no man than this, that a
man lay down his life for his friends.

John 15:13

A true friend never

gets in your way unless you

happen to be going down.

A friend loves at all times,
And a brother is born for adversity.
Proverbs 17:17 NASB

Laughter is the brush

that sweeps away

the cobwebs of the heart.

A happy heart is good medicine
and a cheerful mind works healing,
but a broken spirit dries up the bones.
Proverbs 17:22 AMP

God has a history of

using the insignificant to

accomplish the impossible.

With men it is impossible, but not with God:
for with God all things are possible.
Mark 10:27

People may doubt what you say, but they will always believe what you do.

The tree is known and recognized and judged by its fruit.
Matthew 12:33 AMP

Kindness is a language

which the deaf can

hear and the blind can see.

**His merciful kindness is great toward us:
and the truth of the LORD endureth
for ever. Praise ye the LORD.**
Psalm 117:2

I make it a rule of Christian duty never to go to a place where there is not room for my Master as well as myself.

Don't be teamed with those who do not love the Lord.... How can a Christian be a partner with one who doesn't believe?
2 Corinthians 6:14-15 TLB

Jesus can turn water into wine, but He can't turn your whining into anything.

Do all things without murmurings and disputings.
Philippians 2:14

The smallest deed is better than the greatest intention!

Let us not love [merely] in theory or in speech but in deed and in truth— (in practice and in sincerity).

1 John 3:18 AMP

$\mathcal{I}$ve suffered a great
many catastrophes in
my life. Most of them
never happened.

*God hath not given us the spirit
of fear; but of power, and of love,
and of a sound mind.*
2 Timothy 1:7

*G*uilt is concerned with the past.

Worry is concerned

about the future.

Contentment enjoys the present.

I have learned how to be content (satsified to the point where I am not disturbed or disquieted) in whatever state I am.

Philippians 4:11 AMP

People with tact

have less to retract.

**The heart of the righteous
weighs its answers,
but the mouth of the wicked gushes evil.**
Proverbs 15:28 NIV

Being at peace with yourself is a direct result of finding peace with God.

The peace of God, which passeth all understanding, shall keep your hearts and minds through Christ Jesus.
Philippians 4:7

If you want to make

an easy job seem

mighty hard, just keep

putting off doing it.

How long are ye slack to go to possess
the land, which the LORD God of
your fathers hath given you?
Joshua 18:3

Love sees through

a telescope

not a microscope.

**Love endures long and is patient and kind;
... it takes no account of the evil done to it
[it pays no attention to a suffered wrong].**
1 Corinthians 13:4-5 AMP

Life is not a problem

to be solved, but a

gift to be enjoyed.

**This is the day the LORD has made;
let us rejoice and be glad in it.**
Psalm 118:24 NIV

A pint of example

is worth a barrel

full of advice.

Brethren, join in following my example,
and observe those who walk according
to the pattern you have in us.
Philippians 3:17 NASB

Beware lest your footprints on the sand of time leave only the marks of a heel.

The memory of the righteous will be a blessing, but the name of the wicked will rot.
Proverbs 10:7 NIV

If you were given

a nickname descriptive

of your character, would

you be proud of it?

**A good name is rather to be
chosen than great riches.**
Proverbs 22:1

It's easy to identify people
who can't count to ten.
They're in front of you in the
supermarket express lane.

Be patient with everyone.
1 Thessalonians 5:14 NIV

Tact is the art of

making a point without

making an enemy.

Reckless words pierce like a sword,
but the tongue of the wise brings healing.
Proverbs 12:18 NIV

S*ilence is one of*

the hardest arguments

to refute.

***Whoso keepeth his mouth and his tongue
keepeth his soul from troubles.***
Proverbs 21:23

The best antique is an old friend.

Your own friend and your father's friend,
forsake them not.... Better is a neighbor
who is near [in spirit] than a
brother who is far off [in heart].
Proverbs 27:10 AMP

If you can't feed

a hundred people,

then just feed one.

**As we have therefore opportunity,
let us do good unto all men.**
Galatians 6:10

The trouble with

stretching the truth is

that it's apt to snap back.

A false witness shall not be unpunished,
and he that speaketh lies shall not escape.
Proverbs 19:5

Birthdays are good for you.

Statistics show that

the people who have

the most live the longest.

Teach us to number our days, that
we may apply our hearts unto wisdom.
Psalm 90:12

$\mathcal{F}$aults are thick

where love is thin.

Above all things have fervent charity
among yourselves: for charity
shall cover the multitude of sins.
1 Peter 4:8

The only way to

have a friend is

to be one.

**A man that hath friends must
shew himself friendly.**
Proverbs 18:24

The world wants your best, but God wants your all.

Thou shalt love the Lord thy God with all thy heart, and with all thy soul, and with all thy mind.
Matthew 22:37

$\mathcal{H}$indsight explains the injury that foresight would have prevented.

Do not forsake wisdom,
and she will protect you....
When you walk, your steps
will not be hampered;
when you run, you will not stumble.
Proverbs 4:6,12 NIV

Do not in the darkness
of night, what you'd
shun in broad daylight.

*The night is far spent, the day is at hand: let
us therefore cast off the works of darkness,
and let us put on the armour of light.*
Romans 13:12

$\mathcal{I}$ am defeated, and know it,

if $\mathcal{I}$ meet any human being

from whom $\mathcal{I}$ find myself

unable to learn anything.

*A wise man will hear, and will increase
learning; and a man of understanding
shall attain unto wise counsels.*
Proverbs 1:5

Honesty is the

first chapter of

the book of wisdom.

**Provide things honest in
the sight of all men.**
Romans 12:17

God always gives *His* best to those who leave the choice with *Him*.

Blessed be the Lord, who daily loadeth us with benefits, even the God of our salvation.
Psalm 68:19

A lot of people mistake

a short memory

for a clear conscience.

Herein do I exercise myself, to have
always a conscience void of offense
toward God, and toward men.

Acts 24:16

Faith is not belief without proof, but trust without reservation.

I know whom I have believed, and am persuaded that he is able to keep that which I have committed unto him against that day.
2 Timothy 1:12

A day hemmed in

prayer is less likely

to unravel.

*Pray about everything;... His peace
will keep your thoughts and
your hearts quiet and at rest.*
Philippians 4:6-7 TLB

*W*hen you flee

temptations, don't leave

a forwarding address.

Flee from youthful lusts and pursue
righteousness, faith, love and peace,
with those who call on the Lord
from a pure heart.
2 Timothy 2:22 NASB

A coincidence is a small miracle where God prefers to remain anonymous.

Who can put into words and tell the mighty deeds of the Lord? Or who can show forth all the praise [that is due Him]?
Psalm 106:2 AMP

Sometimes the Lord calms the storm; sometimes He lets the storm rage and calms His child.

The peace of God, which transcends all understanding, will guard your hearts and your minds in Christ Jesus.
Philippians 4:7 NIV

The past should

be a springboard

not a hammock.

This one thing I do, forgetting those
things which are behind, and reaching
forth unto those things which are before.
Philippians 3:13

The teacher asked the pupils to tell the meaning of loving-kindness. A little boy jumped up and said, "Well, if I was hungry and someone gave me a piece of bread, that would be kindness. But if they put a little jelly on it, that would be loving-kindness."

Bless the LORD, O my soul . . .
who crowneth thee with
lovingkindness and tender mercies;
Who satisfieth thy mouth with good things.
Psalm 103:1,4-5

Laughter is a tranquilizer with no side effects.

A merry heart doeth good like a medicine.
Proverbs 17:22

God never asks about

our ability or our inability—

just our availability.

I heard the voice of the Lord, saying,
Whom shall I send, and who will go for us?
Then said I, Here am I; send me.

Isaiah 6:8

*W*hether you think

you can or think you

can't, you're right.

As he thinketh in his heart, so is he.
Proverbs 23:7

$\mathcal{T}$he best way to

cheer up yourself is

to cheer up somebody else.

Give, and it shall be given unto you.
Luke 6:38

Failure isn't falling down.

It's staying down.

A just man falleth seven times,
and riseth up again.
Proverbs 24:16

Nobody can make

you feel inferior

without your consent.

I am fearfully and wonderfully made.
Psalm 139:14

What sir, would the
people of the earth
be without woman?
They would be scarce,
sir, mighty scarce.

As woman came from man,
so also man is born of woman.
But everything comes from God.
1 Corinthians 11:12 NIV

$\mathcal{M}$en have sight;

women insight.

This is my prayer: that your love may abound more and more in knowledge and depth of insight, so that you may be able to discern what is best.

Philippians 1:9-10 NIV

Women are the church's strong rock. As they were the last at the foot of the cross, so they have become the first at the altar.

Charm is deceptive, and beauty is fleeting; but a woman who fears the LORD is to be praised.
Proverbs 31:30 NIV

It was to a virgin woman
that the birth of the
Son of God was announced.
It was to a fallen woman that
his resurrection was announced.

Give her the reward she has earned,
and let her works bring
her praise at the city gate.
Proverbs 31:31 NIV

References

Unless otherwise indicated, all Scripture quotations are taken from the *King James Version* of the Bible.

Scripture quotations marked NIV are taken from the *Holy Bible, New International Version®* NIV®. Copyright © 1973, 1978, 1984 by International Bible Society. Used by permission of Zondervan Publishing House. All rights reserved.

Scripture quotations marked NASB are taken from the *New American Standard Bible.* Copyright © The Lockman Foundation 1960, 1962, 1963, 1968, 1971, 1972, 1973, 1975, 1977, 1995. Used by permission.

Scripture quotations marked AMP are taken from *The Amplified Bible. Old Testament* copyright © 1965, 1987 by Zondervan Corporation, Grand Rapids, Michigan. *New Testament* copyright © 1958, 1987 by The Lockman Foundation, La Habra, California. Used by permission.

Scripture quotations marked NKJV are taken from *The New King James Version* of the Bible. Copyright © 1979, 1980, 1982, 1994 by Thomas Nelson, Inc., Publishers. Used by permission.

Verses marked TLB are taken from *The Living Bible,* copyright © 1986. © 1971. Used by permission of Tyndale House Publishers, Inc., Wheaton, Illinois 60189. All rights reserved.

Scripture quotations marked RSV are taken from *The Revised Standard Version* of the Bible, Old Testament, Section copyright 1980 by the Division of Christian Education of the National Council of the Churches of Christ in the United States of America. New Testament, Section copyright 1979 by the Division of Christian Education of the National Council of the Churches of Christ in the United States of America.

Acknowledgements

Ruth Bell Graham (5), Mother Teresa (6,25,124), Jean Hodges (7), George M. Adams (9), Helen Pearson (12), Joseph Addison (13), Cyrus (14), Henry Ward Beecher (15), G.W.C. Thomas (18), Betty Mills (19), Josh Billings (20,125), Thackeray (21), Joyce Heinrich and Annette La Placa (22), Joyce Earline Steelburg (23), St. Basil (24), Marcus Tullius Cicero, Catherine Graham (40), Lillian Dickson (43), Cervantes (42), Sebastian-Roche (43), Mark Twain (45,109,113,152), William James (46), Zig Ziglar (48), William Feather (49), Bill Cosby (50), Charles Dickens (51), Euripedes (53), Martin Luther King Jr. (54), William Carey (55), Benjamin Franklin (56), Dennis Waitley (59), Mary Gardner Brainard (61), Walt Disney (62), Arnold H. Glasgow (105), Mort Walker (106), Richard Exley (107), John Newton (110), Mark Steele (111), Olin Miller (116), Joseph P. Dooley (119), June Henderson (123), Dr. John Olson (124), Reverend Larry Lorenzoni (129), James Howell (130), Ralph Waldo Emerson (131), Charles H. Spurgeon (134), George Herbert Palmer (135), Thomas Jefferson (136), Jim Elliot (137), Doug Larsen (138), Elton Trueblood (139), Ivern Ball (144), Merceline Cox (146), Henry Ford (148), Mary Pickford (150), Eleanor Roosevelt (151), Victor Hugo (153), Mary Elizabeth Braddon (154), Fulton John Sheen (155).

Additional copies of this book and other titles in
the *God's Little Instruction Book* series are
available from your local bookstore.

God's Little Instruction Book

God's Little Instruction Book for Couples

God's Little Instruction Book for Men

God's Little Instruction Book for Mom

God's Little Instruction Book for Teachers

God's Little Instruction Book for Teens

If you have enjoyed this book,
or if it has impacted your life,
we would like to hear from you.

Please contact us at:

Honor Books
An Imprint of Cook Communications Ministries
4050 Lee Vance View

Colorado Springs, CO 80918

www.cookministries.com